Tribute

THE FIRST COLLECTION

COMPILED BY

Jim & Phil Masterson

ego PUBLISHING ✦ DENVER, COLORADO

Published by EGB Publishing

Photography provided by Bill Reitz and Sue Masterson

Book & Dustjacket design by Bob Schram/Bookends

Tribute

*V*ERY FEW OF US have the opportunity to publicly pay tribute to the people we love, respect and honor. Very few of us win an Academy Award, an Emmy, or a Most Valuable Player award. It seems as though every month or so celebrities have an opportunity to stand at a podium and pay tribute to those who have made a difference in their lives.

My brother and I believe the rest of us, given the opportunity, have tributes we would like to shout from the highest mountain about people we love. About people who have given of themselves. Unfortunately, no one would hear us on the top of a mountain and there would be no cameras or microphones to record our tribute. So there is a need for a book such as *Tribute*.

The authors of the letters in this book express gratitude and love for the people who have made a difference in their lives. We believe that if each of us takes a moment to reflect upon our lives, we can identify people for whom we feel deeply grateful. We are thankful that God has blessed us with their presence in our lives. We cannot imagine our lives without them.

This book provides an opportunity to publicly pay tribute to those special individuals. The sentiments expressed in the letters are sometimes simple, sometimes complicated, but always genuine.

After reading the following letters, we encourage each of you to create your own tributes to those people for whom you are grateful. We have provided blank pages at the end of the book for that purpose.

Contents

BROTHERS & SISTERS

1

SONS & DAUGHTERS

21

HUSBANDS & WIVES

37

MOTHERS & FATHERS

55

FRIENDS & FAMILY

89

GOD & COUNTRY

109

Brothers & Sisters

Dear Brother:

I'm not exactly sure what I want to say, but I'll start by telling you how much I love and respect you. When I look at the photographs of us as children, I can't help but feel so many years were lost. I have chosen, probably for good reason, to block out some of those difficult times.

The problem is that there were good times in those photographs I can't always recall. For a very long time now, I have been trying to make up for that lost time with you. I love being close to you and I think of that often. You are truly my best friend and that is so beautiful because you're my brother as well.

I know I will miss you so very much, but somehow the relationship we have makes your leaving a little easier to live with. It's ironic. Because you mean so much to me, I can feel positive about you leaving.

This is quite an adventure you've chosen for yourself. I know in my heart that you are doing the right thing.

*Yes, you will have doubts but your faith in God will
see you through. Remember that one set of footprints
in the sand.*

*You'll win and lose, succeed and fail, but the key is to
build on the positive and learn from the negative. You
have a great character and that basis will always see
you through. I'm so proud of you, as a man and a
brother. I'll always be here for you, as I know you are
always there for me. As I began, so I end. I love and
respect you.*

Your brother.

Brother,

I can't tell you how much your letter meant to me. It touched me deeply. You are a very sensitive person. I love you. It's good to know I can talk to you. Life wouldn't be the same without you. I love you much.

Your loving sister.

To My Brother,

I don't know where to begin because ever since I can remember you've been there. You have always been a source of strength to me and God only knows how much I've needed that.

Sometimes, I wish we were kids again. I could call you Big Brother, and you could tell me stories about the adventures you've experienced.

I have always looked up to you. You have always been my idol. And I want you to know you still are. The only difference is I now realize just how much I love and respect you. God is our ultimate source of strength, but He realizes we need people along the way. I want to thank you for being there for me. And please know that I'm here for you.

What's great is that things are going well for us all. Things are never perfect but things are good overall. This summer we'll have to go fishing and just talk.

Thanks for being my brother.

To My Big Brother,

On someone's birthday you want to give him a special gift so he knows he is appreciated. The best gift I can give you is my gratitude and respect—both of which I abundantly have for you.

You have been there for me often, sometimes at critical junctures in my life. Without your love and advice my life would undoubtedly be different, to say the least.

The fact is that I can't imagine my life without you. That's how important you are to me. To say thanks hardly seems sufficient. But I am infinitely grateful you are my brother and friend.

Love,

Your little brother.

Sister,

*W*here should I begin? Even since I was young you were by my side. I wish you knew how much you mean to me and I hope you know how much I love you.

You have stood by me through the darkest night and I love you. You are probably the toughest person I know. But you are also the most beautiful.

When God created you, He made the most sensitive, loyal person I know. Look in the mirror and appreciate your beauty.

I know it's difficult but you need to be more selfish. Do what you must do and know that I love you no matter what. And please know that you can call me whenever you want. I think of you often and when I do, I smile because I love you.

Your brother.

Dear Brother,

*M*y fondest memories are those of being a big brother. You were so innocent and handsome. I was so proud. I think one of the most powerful lessons our parents taught us was the value of brothers and sisters. I would do anything for you and I cry as I write this letter to my little brother.

In days gone by, opportunities to show my love for you presented themselves all the time. As you grew into a man the opportunities seemed to be less frequent. That's not anyone's fault; that's just life. But the fire of a big brother still burns inside me as hot as ever.

You're not as innocent today, but I would argue just as handsome as you were so many years ago. I wish there were words to describe how proud I was when your son was born. He is a beautiful little boy and carries the genes of a giant because he is your son. Trust I will always be there for him as I was for you.

Our Lord has special treasures in store for you and your family. You've experienced a great many difficulties in your young life and it's time to enjoy life's sweetness. You've already made great strides in business and most of all as a husband and father. You're truly special and I love you little brother. God has bestowed me a great gift in you. Love to you on your birthday.

Your big brother.

Dear Brother,

My brother, my friend. I am so proud of you and so very happy with you. The first step on the road to a positive fulfilling life is behind you.

You do not have life by its tail. That statement is not for you. Rather, you have life in the palm of your hand. It's up to you what to make of it. Life is not leading you. You are leading life.

It is written, a warrior does not forsake all that he is to satisfy another. Keep your principles above everything. They are what make you special. I love you.

Your brother.

Sister,

I have a lot to say. First, I love you and miss you. I remember when we were little and we would put on skits for Mom and Dad. It is important to remember that because we were both happy and confident.

I really believe that we can both be just as happy and confident today. It takes practice and faith, but I have no doubts. What you have to do is just accept yourself. Sounds easy and it really is you think about it.

You are beautiful and wise. The last few times we talked I was amazed at your wisdom. And believe it or not, I do listen and learn from you. Just take one day at a time and call me on good and bad days both. And just try and accept me. We are all changing and that is good. We won't lose sight of our family. Things change, but our love won't.

Your brother.

Dear Brother,

I was just looking at a picture of the sunset from the deck of your old house. The picture with the weathered tree in it. I found myself wishing I was standing there with you looking at it because I know you'd appreciate that.

I often wish we were kids again just so I could look up to you from a child's perspective. It's so hard for me to describe how much I still look up to you. I know I've said it before, but you'll always be my big brother.

I just thank God I've got you to look towards. I love you and I miss you a lot.

Thanks.

Your brother.

My Sister,

*A*ge is a state of … well, let's just say it's a state. It means nothing and I know you understand that. I am so proud of you as a sister, friend, wife and mother. I don't express it as often as I should, but I love you and cherish the thought of being your brother.

Think of all you are and all that you have accomplished in your life. You should be proud but not content. There is so much left to be done personally and as a player in the big picture. It's exciting!

We need to get the family together more often. It's important and could be a lifesaver for some. A close family gives strength to the individual members. I must go now, but believe me when I say I love you and I am so proud to be your brother.

Your brother.

Dear Brother,

*J*ust a note to say congratulations. It may sound corny, but I just want you to know how proud I am of you. You have always been there for me and you continue to be there for me by providing me with an example to follow with regard to my own career.

More importantly, you provide me with an example of what it is to be a man. A man takes responsibility for his life. A man treats others with dignity and respect. A man appreciates what's given to him. A man never forgets those who have helped him. A man laughs a lot and isn't afraid to cry. A man thanks God for everything because God is the source of all good and has plans for us beyond our comprehension. Thanks for being my brother, friend, and example of what a man is.

Love,

Your brother.

Dear Brother,

I'm at work and I'm thinking how hard it may be for you at times. I just want you to know you're not alone. I love you and will always be your little brother. I'm not trying to give advice, but I was listening to the radio and I thought of you. The Rolling Stones' song says: "You can't always get what you want, but if you try sometimes you'll find you get what you need."

Just keep plugging away and enjoy yourself and I'm sure life will treat you right. You must perceive yourself as you truly are: strong, sensitive, loving, funny, caring, handsome, intelligent, and happy. These things are in you, but it is up to you to believe it. Just be yourself because you'll always be my big brother.

Love and prayers,

Your brother.

My Dear Brother,

You have reached one of those trying times in life, but only one of many to come. High school is for making mistakes. But so is life. For mistakes will become part of your life the same as they have in mine.

Life is a struggle until one gains confidence in one's self and no one can tell you when that will come. Some people reach a confident stage early in life, others do not. Trust me. You are progressing just fine. It is easier for one removed from the scene to see the sun rising in another's life.

Your sun is on the rise. Up to now it has been slowly building. This is your break. You will begin at a new school and will not be stymied at the old school, or in other words, your sun will be allowed to rise at your own pace.

For it is up to you now to show yourself what you can do for we in the family know what you can do and will be proud of you just as we are now. For love and pride are not built on success, but are built on human emotion and feelings. You are a beautiful person. And that is first and foremost, for we in the family love you and will always love you.

My brother, we are at hard times in life now when nothing seems as though it will ever work out. But although it may seem amazing to have it happen when it does, we will feel as though there was nothing but triflings while we struggled to find ourselves. No matter what happens in life, never look back. Look ahead. And be thankful that you are fortunate as we are fortunate to have you as our brother, a loving, thoughtful person. It will take time but all things must pass. So keep busy and try to stop any worrisome thoughts, for life is too short.

Love,

Your brother.

Dear Sister,

I didn't get this card for any particular reason.
I thought it was beautiful and wanted to tell you that
I love you. I also wanted to thank you for all of your
love, advice, attention, and energy over the years.

I was reading a book recently and it was talking about
a person's first memories. One of my first memories is of
you carrying me and dancing around to the soundtrack
from the Unsinkable Molly Brown.

I'm not sure if I really remember this or just imagine it
based on what I've been told. What's important though
is that I "remember" and that it is one of my favorite
memories. The memory means many things to me, but it
also means something to you because it is an example of
your generosity, your caring, your fun, your love.

I guess I'm using this memory as an example from
which to say thank you. Thank you for all of your
love. I am very fortunate and one of the reasons I am
fortunate is that I have you in my life.

Never underestimate your importance in my life, the lives of your immediate family, and the lives of your extended family. I just want you to realize how special you are. Not just for what you do. But for who you are. I would feel blessed just to know you as a friend much less a sister and a friend. I love you and am proud to be your brother and friend.

Dear Sister,

*J*ust a note to say thanks. I can think of no better birthday present than to tell you how thankful I am that you're in my life. I am not alone in feeling blessed to have you as a sister and a friend.

You have always been so wonderful to me. Your sense of humor, patience, advice, and understanding have been blessings in my life. Although I have grown and hopefully matured, I know that the simple love and emotion we have in our lives is what makes life worthwhile. I just want to thank you for so richly blessing my life.

You are a wonderful wife, mother, sister, and friend. In many ways you have been a second mother to me. So I have been twice blessed to have you as a sister and a friend as well.

Happy Birthday,

Your little brother.

Sons
&
Daughters

Happy Birthday My Darling:

Thank you for so many things. Thank you for the happiness you have brought into my life. For all the joy and laughter I've shared with you and your two wonderful children, my grandchildren. And for your dear sweet husband. Such grand memories we have. Thank you.

God has been so kind as to allow me to have you so near, especially at this time in my life. I feel so blessed and thankful for many things.

I love you dearly,

Mom.

Dear Son,

I almost began by writing "My Dear Child."
But you are more than just my child. You are your
mother's son. You're a grandson, a nephew, a cousin,
and a friend. Most importantly, you are a child of God.

Your recent baptism only formalizes what you have
been from the moment of your existence, God's child.
Your Mom and I will do our best to always remember
that God has entrusted us with you.

This is not only a tremendous responsibility, but a
tremendous privilege and honor. If you only knew how
much joy your smile gives us. If you only knew how
much pleasure your voice gives us. If you only knew
how much love your eyes bestow on us.

That's really our task. To let you know and feel how
much we love and appreciate you. I just want to thank
you for the honor of being your Father. I love you.

Dad.

*G*ood Night. Sweet Dreams. See you in the morning!
Thank you little darling, for helping me in the yard.
I couldn't have done it without you.

I love you,

Mom.

My Little Darling Daughter,

*H*ow happy I am that God sent you to me!
I love you so dearly! Always remember that,
my little one. And please always try to do good
and be a good girl as you know how to be.

Sweet dreams—good night—
talk to God and our Blessed Mother—
they always hear you.

Love you,

Mommy.

My Daughter,

*H*appy day of your birth! Just 23 years ago today
God sent me an adorable, tiny, bundle of love and I want
you to know that I am thankful for that little bundle.

I want to thank you for all the love and joy you
brought to me during these 23 years. And I want to
take this opportunity to wish you all the happiness
and joy during your lifetime.

I am thankful that we are friends and I want you to
know I love you very much. You have developed into
a very unique young lady of whom I am very proud.

I feel sure that this year is going to bring you the
happiness and love you truly deserve. I love you.

Mother.

My Darling Daughter,

I had intended getting you a card but decided instead to say a few things I never quite seem to say. Such as: how much love and how much happiness you have brought your Daddy and I in the past 14 years. Because you have, you know. From the time we brought you home from the hospital, a tiny bundle of love, until this very moment, you have filled our lives with pleasantness beyond description.

We have been thankful to be able to give you a Catholic education and to see your love and devotion to our Lady. So it is only in keeping with that love that we ask Her to take care of you in these most important and challenging years.

Just remember never to do anything that you would be ashamed to do in front of Her or our Blessed Lord, and I feel sure you will find all the happiness we wish for you today and always.

And please remember to come to us whenever you need help or comfort because no one in this world loves you as we do. So go now, my darling and grow and develop into a complete and happy adult with our Blessed Lady as your example.

Love and prayers,

Mommy & Daddy.

My Dear Daughter,

You have brought so much joy and happiness into my life since God sent you to me just 21 years ago. I am exceedingly thankful for the many memories I have because of you.

What a little doll you were—a four and a half pound doll and we all had such fun playing with you and loving you. Surely, you can see how happy we all were as you looked through your photo album. I pray that as you look at these happy moments we shared during your years growing up you will feel the love that was always there and still is.

We all love you very much. You are a special and unique person. That is what God intends for you to be, "one of a kind," and that is what you are. I am sorry that you and I have not been as close as I would like us to be. But I am confident that as you grow and become more secure in yourself, we will be even closer than we once were.

You are and always will be very special to me. I want
you always to remember that. I want to thank you for
the happiness and joy you have given me these past 21
years, little darling. I also want you to know I love you
very dearly. I hope your new year will be happy and
fulfilling and that you reach your goals. I love you.

Your mother.

My Dear Daughter,

*W*hat a joy you are to me, my little darling—you made Mother's Day an especially happy one. The dinner in our lovely dining room at our new beautiful table was so delicious. Thank you deeply for a perfect day. I will remember it always.

I have always enjoyed my role in life. Being a mother has been more fulfilling to me than anything I can imagine. I thank God for blessing our home with fine, beautiful children. Children who have given me so much love and joy.

My prayers are with you always. May you find your goal in life, my dearest one. A goal that will give you happiness and always keep you close to our Lord and his blessed Mother. I love you dearly.

Love,

Mother.

My Dear Son,

I want to thank you for being the wonderful son that you are.

You have brought so much joy, pride and love into my life. Besides, you make me laugh—you are fun! And I love that part of you as well.

I am extremely proud of the young man you have become. You have excelled in your profession and gained much respect from your family and your peers. I love you.

Your mother.

Dear Son,

*T*oday we celebrate your first birthday. I have a new appreciation for why we celebrate birthdays. It's to acknowledge the blessing we receive when someone is born into the world.

God blesses mankind with each new person born into the world. There is no doubt God blessed your Mom and I when you were born. I will never forget the power of your existence in our lives—from the moment of your birth.

With your tiny fingers you gripped my finger. The tenderness of your touch cannot be exaggerated. The love in your eyes cannot be underestimated. The sweetness of your voice cannot be over appreciated.

I'll make you one promise on this your first birthday. Your Mom and I will love you always, no matter what life holds for us all. And, although it's difficult for me to imagine, I want you to know that God's love for you dwarfs even the love your Mom and I have for you.

Your godfather once told me, that no matter what happened to me in life, I could always count on God and myself. You too can always count on God and yourself. You can just as surely always count on your Mom and I.

I would be remiss in closing without thanking you. Thank you for your smile, your laugh, the twinkle in your eyes, the melody of your voice. Thank you for being such a blessing.

Dad.

My Children,

*W*hat a wonderful experience it was to spend the weekend with my five beautiful children! It is almost impossible to put into words what it meant to me. The laughter, the sharing of love, the tears, the depth of our feelings! I could feel God's presence.

I'll never be able to thank you enough. It is a memory I shall cherish always. Thank you! God Bless You! I love you!

Mom.

Husbands
&
Wives

On this day, the happiest day of my life came about as I presented my girl with an engagement ring.

There she stood after a hard day's work and although I wanted to say a great deal, words failed me at this time. No man can describe how I felt as the one I admired, loved and forever will, accepted the ring.

Every feature about her, every word she utters, brings forth the sweetness of her character, with the admiration of her greatest admirer, myself.

In her is the unnamed quality that every man admires in his everlasting mother, a quality that she fills beyond compare. I could write pages describing her, but it is senseless as words fail to describe the lovely personage she is. My life is hers, for whom I shall live for. Always kind in my actions, never changing in any way, and resolving to do my utmost to make her happy in every way.

WWII
"A Soldier's Diary."

My Dearest:

*T*hank you for all the love you have given me. I start out each day with the thought that I am loved for who I am. Your love is unconditional and I only hope that I can return it to you. We are about to make it. We have two wonderful children who are always a joy and bring us lots of satisfaction. I love you.

Your husband.

My Dearest,

Just a note to say thanks. Thanks for being you. You are such an inspiration to me. Your faith in God is almost tangible to me as I can feel it. I really enjoy being with you and sharing our lives together.

I respect and admire you just as our children will. I have to admit that sometimes I get frightened at how much you mean to me. But I realize that there is nothing to fear; only something to enjoy and be thankful for.

We are so blessed to have each other and our families and friends. If I take a moment to reflect, I can see the image of God all around me—especially in your eyes. Thanks sweetheart.

Love,

Your husband.

Dear Sweetheart,

Just a note to welcome you home. We missed you tremendously. We missed your sweet voice and your sparkling eyes, which never sparkle brighter than when you look at our son.

Thanks for being such a wonderful mother and wife. I appreciate all of your encouragement and support.

Our son is truly blessed to have such a great mom. Thank you for giving birth and love to such a special child of God.

It seems like a lifetime ago when I could feel him kick and move about in your tummy. God surely loves him and I to have blessed us with someone so special as you.

Love ,

Your husband.

Dear Sweetheart,

I don't know where to begin. But I know that the beginning has to do with you.

It's funny how absence makes the heart grow fonder. You haven't been gone a day and I miss you. I keep reaching out to touch you.

God, I hope you know how much I love you. That's my only fear—that you might not know how much I love you.

I know I tell you thanks pretty often, but I don't know if you realize how much I appreciate your influence in my life. When I think of your beauty, I think of your sweet voice, your soft hair, your radiant smile, your tender hands, and your warm cheeks.

I love you always.

My Dearest,

*T*his ring has as much meaning today as it did on our wedding day. It is a symbol of my undying love for you and our marriage. If there is any difference today versus that special day, December 28, 1985, it would be that I have learned about the beauty of your soul and experienced the tenderness of your heart.

You have shown me the beauty of a rainy day, the silliness of a squirrel at play, the importance of caring for your birds and our two little ducks. You are so very special to God that He has given you the ability to touch nature at its most basic level and that is beautiful. You allow me to be an extension of that experience and I am so thankful.

Your birthday is a great day for me because it represents a day when God delivered you to all of us to know and appreciate. I am so thankful and blessed to be a part of your life. I love you my beautiful wife and I cry today for the joy you give me each day. Happy Birthday!

Your husband.

Dear Sweetheart,

Where should I begin? Perhaps at the beginning because I feel as though I've known you all of my life. From the first breath I drew, I've dreamt of you and all that you are. When I hear that song which says "Whom shall I send Lord? Is it I Lord?" I feel you. I feel your essence, your beauty, your love.

You are the truest person I've ever known. I can't believe my dream has come true. You're my dream, my reality, my love. God only has words to express how much I love you. I can't begin to do justice to you. To describe your generosity. Your kindness. Your innocence.

I wish I were a painter because then at least I could begin to describe you in picture. I'd first paint the majesty of the mountains. Then I'd paint the purity of the blue sky. Next, I'd paint the softness of the clouds. Finally, I'd paint the warmth of the sun.

Thank you sweetheart. I love you.

Dearest,

I'm sitting here on the plane melancholy because I miss you so much already that my heart aches. I wanted to write you a letter and all I have is this airbag. Ha. Ha.

But I can't wait to tell you what an incredible time I had with you. I felt so complete with the mountains and your family. You will never know what an incredible blessing you have been in my life.

I can't write this letter without being overcome with emotion. I love you so much I can't believe it's my heart and that I could love anyone this much. You are so much a part of me, I feel incomplete when you are not with me.

I can't tell you how excited I am about our future. No matter what life holds for us, I know one thing for sure—I will always love you. Being with you is the most incredible gift God could ever give me. I only hope I make you as happy as you make me. I thank God for you every day.

All my love, Your wife.

My Dearest Wife,

I couldn't find the right card this year that expressed the feeling I have for you on this very special day. So I decided to go back to the old 10+10 method that we learned so long ago.

As I watch our children grow I am truly amazed at them. I know there are times they are not the best, but the majority of the time they are the greatest kids in the world. Your constant work with them really shows. Sure I can teach them how to throw a ball or shoot a basket, but the things you have been teaching them will last them a lifetime. I know one day they will look back and say with confidence that their mother really did a great job and loved them for being themselves. Our children are extremely lucky that they have you for a mother and I am extremely lucky that I have you for a wife and best friend. So on this special day, take a special thanks from us for being you.

All my love and prayers.

Your husband.

"*No one could ever fill your shoes.*"
I saw this phrase and immediately thought of you.
I never dreamed you would walk into my life and make
it so complete. I just wanted you to know what an
incredible blessing and gift you are in my life. Sometimes
words are not adequate to express my feelings, but I
wanted you to know how truly special you are to me.

Love,

Your sweetheart.

To My Wife,

How can I express all the love I have for you in my heart? Certainly words can in no way begin to scratch the surface. Is it possible with a tender hug meant only for you or a soft kiss with your name imprinted upon my lips? Could it be with a show of understanding in a difficult situation or a joyful smile given to you when you are blue? A strong shoulder for you to lean on or a soft shoulder for you to rest your beautiful head upon? Some say the eyes are the window to the soul. I believe the eyes are a reflection of the heart and when mine gaze upon you, peace and happiness runs over. Thank God you were born June 25th.

Love,

Your husband and best friend.

My Dearest,

*A*s I lie here in bed thinking of you, I realize how fortunate I am to share my life with you. It seems as though I've known you my whole life and that feels very reassuring. After we got off the phone tonight I realized how much we are alike and have in common. And for that we are blessed.

I just want you to know that sharing my life with you is the most important thing to me. I also want you to know how much I admire you—your strength, integrity, generosity, spirituality, and beauty. When I think of you, I think of God because I know how much you love Him. Your faith is probably the quality that most attracted me to you. That and your breathtaking beauty.

I'll never forget you walking down the stairs of your parents' home on our wedding day. That is the only time in my life that I can recall having my breath taken away.

Your faithful husband.

My Dear Wife,

*J*ust a note to say I love you and miss you even
though you've been gone all of ten minutes.

It's hard for me to tell you just how much I love you.

Every time I think of you, I think of how much God
loves you. How you're such a beautiful creation of His
and how blessed I am to have you as my wife and friend.

Thanks for everything.

Dearest One,

I'm sitting here ready for bed after having an absolutely fabulous wedding shower with good friends. I wanted to write you a note to thank you for being such a blessing in my life. I received a lot of advice tonight, but the one that stands out is your sister's advice. She said to remember that you are marrying your best friend.

I feel so incredibly complete every time I think of you and when we are together. I truly see God when I think of us together as husband and wife. I want you to know how happy you have made me and how proud I will be to be your wife. I'm excited to walk through life with you and experience the down times as well as the joyous ones. I feel truly blessed and just wanted to thank you and for you to know that I'll always be there for you.

Your wife to be.

My Dear Wife,

You are my station in life. What I have always
wanted, I have found in you.

Love, tenderness, friendship, trust, respect. The list
is endless!

I love you so much.

Your husband.

To My Wife,

We have each other and we're in love. What more is there when you stop and think about it. I believe in you and I believe in our dream.

Love always,

Your husband.

Mothers
&
Fathers

Dear Mom,

I just wanted to take this opportunity to tell you how much I love you. I know I've said that often, but it's hard to imagine saying it too often. I just hope that my actions have reflected my words and thoughts half as much.

I know your actions have reflected your words of love for each of us. We can never thank you for all your love and sacrifice throughout our lives, but I want to thank you nonetheless. As I've said before, all of my success, now and in the future, is a credit to you and the atmosphere you created for me.

Never forget that our love for you is only a minor reflection of God's love for you.

Your son.

Dear Dad,

I would like to take this time to thank you so very much for all your help, support, and love.

It's what I need at down times and that's when it came through the strongest.

I often forget to say these three simple words—I love you.

But I want you always to know I love you much more than you can imagine.

You're the greatest dad and I just can't say I love you enough. I don't know what I would do without you.

Your daughter.

Dear Mom,

$\mathcal{Y}$ou don't know how much your letter meant to me.
This experience has changed me forever. I love you more
than ever. There is so much I want to say, but I just
can't put it into words. I, too, enjoy our time spent
together. But three words describe how I feel when
I'm with you, I love you. I am so thankful for you
and Dad. I don't know how I'd survive without you.

Your daughter.

Dear Mom,

*J*ust a note to thank you for all your love and generosity
over the years. Some say that love is attention, energy and
time spent with an individual. If that is true, then you're
without a doubt one of the most loving people on earth.
You have always given each one of us your undivided
attention and the full benefits of your energy. I hope we
in turn have loved you as much as you deserve.
Thank you, Mom.

I love you.

Your son.

Dear Mom,

*W*here should I begin? I guess I should say thanks first. Thanks for being the light of my life. You have been my friend as well as my mother. I was the happiest child I could be, thanks to you! And now I am a happy adult.

It hasn't been easy for me but with a family led by you and good friends I have made it through all difficult times. More importantly, God has seen me through it all. And your example of faith has helped me many a time.

I used to wish things to be so different for you. I used to even wish you had never married Dad. That you found someone who made you really happy.

But where would we, your children, be? I hope we have all given you happiness because we all love you so much. I have stopped wishing for things like that. I have my goals and I will work towards them with God's guidance. I read a nice phrase recently, "Not mine but Thy will be done."

Mom, you have trusted God through so many tragedies that it amazes me. But that trust has enabled you to be happy. You truly are a great example to follow. I hope I someday meet someone I love as much as you. I would be lucky twice in a lifetime.

I love you.

Your son.

P.S. You are the most beautiful lady I know.

Dear Mom,

I would never have made it this far if not for all the lessons you taught me early and often.

When I feel down or tired, I try and think of you, Mom. You inspire me and give me hope. I love you so much.

Love,

Your son.

Dear Mom and Dad,

*T*hank you for loving and caring for me!!! I love you so very much!! I hope that we will never lose each other. I love you and God Bless You!

Love,

Your son.

If I were to think of a word to replace the word
"Father" it would be . . .

> Caring,
>
> Loving,
>
> Generous,
>
> Sharing,
>
> Compassionate,
>
> Peaceful,
>
> Patient,
>
> Trustworthy.

But after I thought this through and through,
I decided I would name it you.

> Love,

> Your daughter.

Mom,

I can always count on you to be there. There is so much I have to be thankful for and the best way I can express this thanks is the following:

On this day, Mother's Day, I shall do my best to be a motherly person unto to you as your mother was to you and you are to me.

A Mother is a person who loves,
A Mother is one who cares,
A Mother is an angel sent from Heaven,
She is devoted and willing,
Always ready to go out of her way.

Someday I want to be a Mother just like you.

Your daughter.

Dear Mom,

I realized recently what one of the gifts you have given me as one of your children. You have taught me to be an owner not a victim! Through all your life and its trials, you were never a victim. You never let life do that to you and I promise to follow your teachings. I love you, Mom.

Happy Birthday!

Your middle son.

Dear Mom,

You always have been my protector. Whatever action you needed to take to make me grow up, it was a great action to take. Thank you for being there for me. I love you with all my heart.

Your son.

Dear Mom,

*M*issing any Mother's Day is difficult, but this one more so than others. I wish I was there to celebrate with you, but I will be home shortly after Mother's Day.

I just wanted you to know how much I appreciate all of your love and generosity over the years. I know you wish you had a million dollars to give each one of us, but I hope you know that you've given us more than money could ever buy.

You are a great mom and a wonderful person. One of the joys of getting older is that I can appreciate you as a person in addition to you being my mom.

I have to say that I admire you both as a mom and as a woman. Thanks for all your love. I hope we have returned some of that love.

Your son.

Dear Mom,

*E*very day brings loving thoughts of you. A smiling face and helpful ways. Today I'm in college and almost 20 years old because of you. My love for you is over-flowing and always remember, I never fail to love you more each day.

Love always,

Your son.

Dear Mom,

My body and my mind tell me I'm a thirty-year-old man but my heart tells me I'm just a little boy who still needs the love and wisdom of his mother.

Life can be such a struggle at times, but as long as we don't lose track of what's important we will prevail. It's family that counts and you are the central figure in this family. I love you so very much and I need you as much today as I did 30 years ago. Just in different ways.

Love,

Your son.

Dear Mom,

*L*ook around the dinner table at your family. You are responsible for giving us life and love. Thank you for all we have become.

Love,

Your son.

Dear Mom,

*T*hank you for everything you have done for us.
You can count on all of us in taking care of you.
We love you very much and are proud of you.
Hope you have a wonderful day!

Love,

Your daughter.

Mom,

*E*veryone has their own idols or someone they look up to, but I need no one but you. Who could have a better example to follow than someone who has been touched by God himself? From here on in life, I am going to try to mold myself to act and be more like you. I will learn to enjoy life everyday and find something in each person that is good because, after all, we are all made in our Lord's image. I love you so very much and appreciate the example you have set for all of us to follow.

Your grateful son.

Dear Mom,

I just wanted to take a moment to let you know how much I love you.

When I think back to when I was a child, I have some great memories. I remember us having lunch (pepperoni sandwiches), walking to the shopping center, walking to school, and you reading to me before naps.

It's hard to grow up when you are so happy and secure. But that is what life is all about—growing, changing, and experiencing. God loves us and has a plan for us. We are part of His plan.

I just want you to know how much you mean to me. I miss you so much and I do wish once in awhile we could turn back time.

You have taught me a lot. Be positive. Smile. Trust. Love. Happiness. Faith. Friendship. Mom, I love you and you are always in my thoughts and prayers.

Your son.

Dear Mom,

*T*his is something I wrote while you were away.

I really miss you. I love you a great deal. It's amazing
that after all these years, I still love you as much as
I always have. God surely must love me to have given
me such a wonderful mom.

I don't know how to say thanks. But I was thinking if I
were a father, I would want my child to be happy, content,
and have other qualities I consider important like honesty,
loyalty, and kindness. I think that if I can try to have
those qualities, it might be some way of saying thanks.
I believe that I do display those qualities and I am happy.
So I guess I'm trying to say thanks in the best way I can.

Thanks for making the commitment and loving me
always. You are the best and I hope you know that.
If I can only be a little bit like you, I'll surely go far.

Love,
Your son.

Dear Mom,

How can I thank you for all you have given me
all of these years? Ever since I was a child you have
watched over me and given me all of your love.

I remember all the times we walked home from school.
I remember one day in particular. You pointed out a
robin washing itself in the rainwater that ran down the
sidewalk. You have helped me appreciate God's creation.
And that's why I appreciate you. Oh, Mom sometimes
I would give anything to be that kid again walking
home with his best friend, you!

Life can be sad sometimes, but you have taught me to have
faith in God. You really have been inspirational to me.

I guess the best way I can thank you, is to tell you that
I am happy. Thanks to you.

I will always work hard to make you proud of me and
I will always be your son. Oh, Mom, I love you!

Your son.

Dear Mom,

*H*appy Birthday. I know this is a milestone in
your life. But you are just as beautiful and caring as
you always have been. I thank you for all that you
have given me over the years. I would not have gotten
so far in school without your help and encouragement.
Your attitude lifts me everyday to do my best and to
strive for my goals. I love you very much. Have a
great "29th" year.

Love,

Your son.

Dear Mom,

Many a morning I walk to the bus, not always wanting to. But as I look around and see the mountains, the sun, the clouds, and the blue sky, I thank the Dear Lord who has placed me here. Then I think about who I learned that from and I quickly thank Him for the woman that will always be the light of my life.

Love,

Your son.

Dad,

*You're the best father anyone could have!
That's why today is a special day. It honors you,
a great father. Thank you for working so hard so we
can eat, vacation, go to school, go on shopping sprees!
I love you a lot.*

Your little daughter.

My Mother's Hand,

*M*om, your hands are soft and beautiful. I like your hands a lot. They are nice to hold. They are hard-working hands. I know you like to work in the yard. You do a great job!

Love,

Me!!

Mom,

*A*s the money is tight here, I thought I'd write a letter on plain old paper rather than buy a card to tell you Happy Birthday.

I also thought I would take the time to thank you for all you have done for me. I think about that a lot.

All the sacrifices you make so that I can go to school here. I can't say thank you enough. I look forward to Sunday nights when I get to call. Every time I get off the phone I wish to see you more often. I love you all so much. In a way it took me leaving to realize exactly how much I love all of you.

I guess I better stay out here so it remains that way. Just kidding! Well, I better go study. But thank you again and Happy Birthday. I love you and miss you.

Love always,

Your daughter.

Dear Mother,

It's time for me to leave and I want to thank you for all of your love. This love has given me every opportunity for happiness. Now I must go and create my own happiness.

When you think of me, don't feel anxious. Feel content that you have prepared me in such a way that I am able to experience all that is healthy and natural. And when you think of me and my eventual success, be proud of yourself because the credit goes to you and the atmosphere you provided for me.

I know you will miss me as I will miss you. But try to focus on the love we have for one another because I too will struggle to only concentrate on the love I have for you.

Your loving son.

Mom and Dad,

*T*here are many reasons I wanted to give you this card. To wish you a Happy Mother's Day and Father's Day and to thank you for everything— especially your support and for allowing me to stay at school this summer because I know how much change this summer will bring. I wanted to tell you that despite your concerns, you have given my brother and I every- thing that we have ever needed and wanted. My brother will be successful in life because you both have prepared him for real life. No amount of money in the world can equal that preparation and your unconditional love. Looking back, there is nothing I would have changed about my childhood. What we make of ourselves in the future will not come as a result of what you provided us with materially, but rather the values you instilled in us—which are too numerous to count.
Thank you for that.

It's hard to believe that I finished my sophomore year already. Time goes so fast and I am so grateful for the

*time I have to spend with you. It's that time and the
happiness it brings that matter in life. My experiences
at school have taught me that because that love is what
I took to school with me and what my brother will take
with him. I know that his leaving will be difficult for
you, but as you both told me through all the difficult
times in my life, change makes us stronger people. Your
love helped me through so much. Thank you. I love you
both and miss you so much. Happy Mother's Day
and Father's Day.*

Love always,

Your daughter.

Dear Mom and Dad,

*W*ell, I guess you guys just arrived home from taking me to school. Thanks for the lift!

I was standing in front of the mirror and I uttered to myself, "Here goes round two." I've seen what college life is like and I love it. I'm having a great time. I was given such a great opportunity.

I was talking to someone and they commented how lucky I have been to be given an enormous opportunity to go to college and have these experiences. I said that I was, and that this is all due to my parents. I have received everything from you two.

You taught me respect, my work ethic, caring, sharing, and most of all, love. Love is such an important thing for success. You two have guided me to the top with love and have provided me with an opportunity to reach the top. Thank you! I can't say these two words enough! Thank you! I love you very much. Thank you for all you have provided for me.

Love,
Your daugther.

Dear Mom and Dad,

On Christmas morning I shall receive Holy communion for your special intention. I shall ask the infant Jesus to shower his blessings upon you. I deeply appreciate all you have done for me and shall implore the newborn babe of Bethlehem to give me the grace to do everything to make you proud of me. Wishing you both a Happy and Holy Christmas and a New Year filled with peace and joy.

Your loving child.

Dear Dad,

Well, this is the fourth time that I've written this note so I should be pretty good at it. There is so much that I want to tell you and I just don't know how. I love you and I wish I could tell you more often. A lot has gone on in my life this year and you have stood by me. Thank you for letting me switch schools even though I know you still don't understand why. Thank you for letting me reach out and explore the different options in my life.

After all Dad, we cannot expect to find new beaches if we are afraid to lose sight of the shore. I know that in time the right job for you will come along. You have to remember that "Some of God's greatest gifts are unanswered prayers." I think Garth Brooks wrote that song just for us. You have always provided me with everything I need. I love you. Happy Father's Day.

Love,

Your little girl.

Dear Mom,

On my daughter's third birthday, I wanted to write you and thank you for being my mom. You are so very dear and good and loving and beautiful.

As I watched my daughter today, I felt so much love and joy in my heart, and now I know how you felt with each one of us, your children.

I only wish I would have appreciated you as a child as much as I do now, but I know that isn't how life is.

I hope you know how much I love you. Missing you isn't so hard because you are so dear to my heart and with me in spirit and thought every day! I love you.

Your daughter.

Friends
&
Family

Dear Friend:

*I*t's late at night. And as I lie in bed pondering what life is all about, as I often do, I am reminded of my friends.

Not everyone I know is a "friend." A friend is someone who I've laughed with many times while discussing women, sports, school, etc. Many times, too, I've cried with my friends—life, death, women. I'm sure we've covered every topic under the sun. This too I am certain of, there will be many more topics to come.

I don't know what prompted me to write this letter, short as it is. I guess only to say thank you—friend. Talk to you soon.

Love,

Your friend.

Dear Friend,

*Thanks for calling me to tell me about your dad.
It meant a hell of a lot bro. I tried to call you today,
but no answer. I am so sorry, but actually it's for the
best. I know deep inside you loved him a lot. I know it
must be hard for you. For it was hard for me.*

*You see, I remember him as a great man, a man respected
by all. He was the first man, besides my father and
grandfather, that I ever looked up to. Beyond that,
he was the first man I had deep respect for. A respect
that will always be with me.*

*As a senior now, I can picture him at our first football
practice, even the first time he ever made the team hit a
knee in front of the grotto. He made a deep impression on
my life. I've wanted to go by and see him just to talk, to
try and help him. I never did, and now that hurts because
maybe I could've helped. I know you wanted to help him
and I know it meant a lot to him. But it would've taken a
miracle to change a smart, hard Irishman like him. But
he knew that you loved him and that's what counts.*

I know that all who came in contact with him respected him. All who played ball against him in the old days respected him. He died a hard death, but will suffer no more. For he was with God throughout his life and he will walk with him now. He died for a reason. Whether it's for one person or 100, he suffered so that people like me won't wreck their lives on alcohol. I hope his cause will be known by all who looked up to him and respected him, most of all by the one who is so like him. The one who is proud and strong and intelligent like him. That is why you two had a hard time communicating. You are made of the exact materials as your dad, the best of qualities.

I pray that I may never take a fall like he did, and know that as long as I pray and remember him, I never will. Above all, I pray that you will follow in his footsteps, that is, the footsteps of years gone by. And never take a fall. You also will be respected by all and the family name will always be as strong and proud as it always has been. And you can make it grow in his memory.

He had to have been the best of men to win a woman so lovely as your mom and together the family they had.

*He died, but his name will live on. I wish I could have
been at the funeral, but it really would have choked me up.*

*Well, I really don't know what else to say. This probably
makes no sense. But maybe you understand. It's just that
I respected him and the last time I saw him, it hurt.
But I only remember him as he was before his disease
changed him.*

*Promise me as a bro that if I ever start to fall, you'll
help me back up. For I know I'll help you if it's one
year or thirty years from now. I'll help you with
an open heart and a lot of leather in your butt.*

Take care, bro.

Happy Birthday Friend,

It's been a long time since I've had someone I could call my best friend—someone who is always understanding, patient and, especially, kind. I feel so blessed to say you're it. How lucky I am.

Love,

Your friend.

Dear Friend,

*T*his has been a year of many joys and surprises. One of them was having a friend like you. I was glad to find your support in what your daughter and I have decided to undertake this coming year. She means so much to me and knowing you are behind us is a great blessing.

This year is full of goals, dreams and the excitement of starting a business. It is a great hope. Thank you for your help in keeping my dreams alive.

For this Christmas I can only offer my skills and give you the gift of myself and all the friendship you've given me. My gift for you this year is my service. Any repairs or work needing my services, I will be there for you. Thanks for a great year.

Your friend.

*I*t's time for my departure from the staging area for my trip overseas. Sad indeed. Sad, for now I leave my brother, his wife and their baby. How wonderful they were to me and my girl when she spent the wonderful days she did with me. Days that shall forever live within me and how I hope that God will spare me to once again look upon her lovely countanance. May God keep her and should I not return, may the one who marries her be the best for indeed he shall have the best girl in the world. Keep her I pray with tears in my eyes as I love her so deeply as you know so well and how I long to have her with me always.

Tears fill my eyes as I write these lines, well-deserved ones for I leave behind me the best mother and father known to this world. Sorry I am for the tears I may have caused them, and may my part in this war be for them. I shall forever try to make them proud of me.

Yes, how clearly I see my family before me. I ache with every thought of leaving them now, hoping it will not be forever.

*Still, I face that which lies before me with every
confidence in the world for I know their prayers shall
be mine, the only thing that shall help me return.
God be with me and my loved ones always.
Keep them well and keep me for them.*

WWII
"A Soldiers Diary."

*J*ust a few minutes ago I bid my brother, his wife and
their son goodbye. Yes, my brother cried as did I, for I
know of no two brothers closer than we. Yes, he knows the
odds as I do and I hope his departure will be some time off.
Oh how good that little family looked for in them our
family tradition is to go on with their son the representative
of us. May he grow to be a wonderful man. I never had
the chance to bring my own into this world and, should
I not return, be in him what I longed to be.

Wonderful memories I leave behind. So long Mom and
Dad. So long dear brother. And so long Sweetheart.
I love you oh so much and shall forever. Yes, this diary
is for you to remember me by and, from within the lines
written here you shall know the love I have for you that
no other man could equal. I shall be with you on this
earth always and forever in heaven. So long.
Thanks for that kiss.

WW II
"A Soldiers Diary."

To My Dear Family,

*T*hank you for all your love and understanding over the years.

I just wanted to tell you how proud I am to be from this family.

The thought of us together forever is the warmest feeling I could ever have.

I love every one of you. Thanks for all your love.

Happy St. Patrick's Day!

Your sister and daughter!

To My Family,

*T*hank you for being so understanding with me
through all these years. I really appreciate having you
as my family. I am really sorry for having done so
many wrong things in my life. I just wanted to tell
you all that I love you and will always love you.

I hope as the years go on that we learn to love ourselves
and each other more and more. Thanks for being my
family, especially you, Mom. Thank you!

Love,

Your daughter and sister.

Dear Family,

I sure don't know where to begin. There have been
so many trials and tribulations, laughs and smiles,
I don't know whether to laugh or cry. But the fact is
that I am crying. I am crying because my love for you
and my gratitude for your love is deep. I tell you, being
in this family truly has been a blessing. I thank God
for each of you.

The years haven't been easy, but we have persevered and
succeeded. I am convinced that no matter how tough
things get if you trust in God, everything will be fine.
I read the following quote once, "Tough times don't last,
tough people do." More than being tough we have been
trusting, faithful people. After 23 years, I just want to say
thanks and I love you. I have enjoyed being everyone's
little brother and Mom's son. We are a fortunate family.

Your youngest son and brother.

Dear Family,

*A*s I sit here and look at old photos I realize I am indeed lucky. I had such a good time growing up with you all. When I look at these pictures, even the bad times, I see God in each of us and all around us. He really does love us and He loves Dad too. The tough part is, Dad fell out of the picture. He fell out because he lost faith. He didn't trust that God and his family loved him, and God only knows we did.

I will never understand why Dad left us as he did, but I don't think I should be concerned about it. I just know that we all loved Dad and that he is now receiving God's wondrous love. In a lot of ways, he is lucky, but boy did he miss out on a good time with us. And that's exactly what we need to do, enjoy each other. Life is short. So let's make the most of it and each other.

It's important for me to let you know that I love you. I'm sure you're aware of it, but I wanted to remind you. Thanks for everything over the years.

Your son and brother.

Dear Family and Friends,

To my loving family that has provided guidance and strength in my life.

I am writing you today to tell you about my experience trying out for a Division One baseball team. The reason that I chose to thank all of you is that each person has inspired, taught and guided me in the game I love so much.

My baseball career ended today. I cannot describe the emotions that run through my mind right now. There is anger, sadness, and happiness. When I had my first tryout, I had an unsettled feeling in my stomach. I came to find out later what that feeling was.

It was that I had not shown what I could fully do with my potential. I hit the baseball very well, and my fielding was great. I first thought my uneasiness was my illness that I had the day of tryout, but it wasn't. It was like I was afraid to let go and show the coaches all that I am. I'll tell you what, I felt confident that day after I left the field. Not that I would make the team, but at the fact that I had worked hard. And you know what, I got called back the next day to hit on the field for the coaches.

When I walked onto that field the second day, a feeling like no other sunk in. The complete baseball atmosphere was right there in front of me. Balls were flying, people were yelling, and players were having fun. This is a feeling that I cannot describe. I had a smile on my face the whole practice. I wondered what the other guys were thinking. This place was where I had dreamed of being, and now I was there. I was in the most special place in the world. I was trying out for a Division One ball club!! How much better could it get? I passed the test I set for myself. I was hesitant about trying out all summer, but I did it and it felt great! I wouldn't trade that second practice for anything in the world.

I thank my batting coach and friend. You've taught me well, bud. You gave me inspiration and perspective that my family couldn't provide. Thank you for everything you have done to make my dreams come true!

Dad, you taught me this game. From day one, you were my coach, my idol. You brought baseball to my life. I love you, Dad! Thank you for allowing me to grow under your guidance.

Mom, what can I say about you? You were my guide through the tough times. While I was trying to tough out an injury or other situation, you were the person to come to and cry when I needed it. You and Dad are the world to me. I love you guys so much! You have given me the world. Thanks for teaching me to fly!

My big sister, always leading the way only to be followed by her little bro. You have set such a good example for me. One of the reasons I chose to come to school here was because you were here, and I knew it would be twice as good if you were here. You are my true best friend in life. Thank you.

To my extended family, you have shown me the true meaning of family. All of you have shown me new light and paths toward success. I love you all very much.

One thing that I have learned from this is that all of us must reach for our dreams. You know what my dream is? My dream is to play Division One baseball. You know what, I got that dream. I was out on a perfect field, on a perfect afternoon, and I was playing baseball. Though I am sad my career as a baseball player is over, I am happy. When a person reaches their dream, it is so sweet. Thank you everyone, and I love you. Baseball ended for me today. What a great feeling!

Love,

Your son, brother, grandson, nephew, and friend.

Dear Family,

I was just thinking about gifts to give each of you so that you would know that I was thinking about you. Just a little something to let you know that I love you. Then I realized how temporary that is. Things get old, worn out, and sometimes break. But not my love for you.

The more I progress, the more I realize how blessed I am. How wonderful to know that you are loved. How peaceful it is to know that my love for you has never changed. My love for you has been constant.

God's love for us is constant, and I am glad that I can share in that love.

Your son and brother.

God
&
Country

A Tribute to God

You've given me a lot to be grateful for. I have a wonderful family, many good friends, and teachers who help me learn my lessons well. I thank you for the wonderful although sometimes troublesome world in which I live. And I am grateful for the solid ground you have given me to walk on. But the one thing I am most grateful for is you, my God, in Whom I can confide, trust and love and be me, the person I really am.

Love,

One of Your Children.

A Response from God

I am happy that you are grateful and thankful for the things I have given you. I thank you for trusting in me and letting me know you love me, trust me and are able to confide in me. I love you little one and I shall give you honor. And I hope you will do the same for me. My little one, you are special and I have never and will never make anyone like you. I will give you what I feel is necessary!

Love,

God.

Dear God,

Today is the beginning of the rest of my life. As I look around this house, I remember some bad times and good times as well. But today I choose to remember the good times. The many laughs, hugs, and smiles.

We have indeed prevailed. You have seen us through it all. Sometimes walking beside us, sometimes holding our hand, and other times carrying us.

We need only trust in you. We made it. Thanks! I love you.

What a life! Just when a guy thinks all the world is against him, God shows him the way through the darkness. He begins to believe in himself and life, and then God blesses him with a gift.
God gives him a companion, a wife, a friend.

A Thankful Husband.

*H*ome again, to a place I thought I'd not see for some time. Home to the Mom and Dad I love so dearly. Home to the places I'll never forget, and home to the buddies I know so well. Happy? No other man could have been happier.

What a change it was to come home a soldier about to learn the job set out for me to do my part in winning the war of nations. Yes, I walked up and down the streets I once walked as a young squirt. In every window or door I stopped to knock at, a flag with perhaps two or three stars on it, brought home to me that Joe O'Leary, Tom Fox, Hank Knilling, Ed Hupp, Paul Weadick, and many others were gone as I had gone, to fight the battle in defense of this ever-glorious country of ours.

As I stopped at each home, smiles broader than usual greeted me for there I stood as someday their loved ones would stand at home again. They changed very much for their hair had become gray and their faces still with fright, praying and hoping more than before.

It was now more than ever did I feel as though I was
out of place. For here I was home while others were afar.
May God hasten this victory so that all of us can be
home to the ones we love so dearly.

WW II
"A Soldiers Diary."

Dear Reader,

*T*HANKS FOR TAKING THE TIME to read *Tribute*.
We appreciate you spending your hard earned
money and hope that it inspired you to pay
tribute to the special people in your lives.

If you have a tribute (whether it be a
poem, letter or diary excerpt) you would like
included in a future volume of *Tribute*, please
send your tribute to:

8174 *South Holly Street, Suite* 419
Littleton, Colorado 80122
or *tribute_2000@Yahoo.com*

If your tribute is included in a future volume,
your contribution will be acknowledged and you
will receive a copy of the volume as our thanks.
Feel free to include tributes to family, friends,
teachers, coaches, veterans, God, and country.

Thanks,

Jim & Phil Masterson

Tribute

My Special Tributes

Tribute

My Special Tributes